Stewardship: Managing Your Life Through God's Perfected Pattern

By: Burnell Williams, Jr.

Stewardship: Managing Your Life Through God's Perfected Pattern

By Burnell Williams, Jr.

ISBN-13: 978-0692356241

Scripture quotations noted HCSB are from the Holman Christian Standard Bible © 1999, 2000, 2002, 2004 by Holman Bible Publishers.

Scripture quotations noted KJV are from the King James Version © 1984, 1991 by AMG International, Inc.

Unger's Bible Dictionary. 3rd Ed. © 1966 Moody Publishers 1988.

Dr. Cindy Trimm quotations from Glad Tidings Newspaper Nov/Dec 2010.

<u>**Dedication**</u>

To my wonderful wife Alicia, you've stuck beside me with unparalleled encouragement and support. I couldn't have become the man I am without you and your love.

To my daughters and inspiration, Azariah and Micaela, I love you princesses.

A lot of people want more in life, however the more you have, the more you are held responsible for. In essence, you have to know what to do with what you have. A lot can be said about life experiences, but every now and then it is a good idea to sit down and read a book. Books that can help you gain more knowledge, more wisdom and more understanding. In his book, Stewardship: Managing Your Life Through God's Perfected Pattern my dear friend Elder Burnell Williams, Jr. gives step-by-step tools on Stewardship and living your life the way that God intended.

The book is broken down into four different sections. Each section is written in a conversational manner. The chapters are precise and to the point as they provide knowledge in areas that impact the average person's day-to-day life.

Immediately following the Intro, Stewardship of the Steward is where Elder Burnell Williams, Jr. jumps right in by putting things into perspective in regards to self. It is so easy to point out the flaws in others, but it isn't until those flaws are found in self-reflection where true deliverance and change can come. If one is to be the best form of him or herself that they can be, it is essential to be the best steward over one's self as possible. Concepts such as work, education, time management, health, and money management, just to name a few, are all addressed in the very first section of Stewardship: Managing Your Life Through God's Perfected Pattern. The first portion alone will immediately capture your attention and leave you wanting to read more.

Family Management is the second section where every area of the family is touched on including husbands, wives, sons, daughters and just the overall family structure. Oftentimes, it comes easy for a person to focus on the outside dynamics of life i.e., work or ministry but the foundation of everything starts in the home. If the home structure is not in place, the total make-up of the individual can never be complete.

If you desire to be a leader or already play that role, you will find great gain in the third section of Stewardship: Managing Your Life Through God's Perfected Pattern. Whether it is your community, your church, your friendships or your work there are many areas in life to consider as a leader.

In my opinion, the most important, yet often overlooked, test of true leadership is character. Character cannot be earned. It does not have a dollar amount attached to it. Character is who you are on the inside out. Traits such as integrity, discipline, loyalty, and honesty all make up an individual's character. In addition, Godly leadership must take on the character of Christ. If you refer to the New Testament in the Bible you can easily see how Jesus led by example. Yes, He spoke to the people, but I believe that His actions spoke even louder. The true test of great leadership is how closely they emulate our Lord and Savior. Many are called, but few are chosen. When you see a great leader, know that he or she is definitely one of the chosen ones.

The last section of the book touches on spiritual stewardship. This section of the book is simply amazing. While reading, I guarantee your whole entire mindset will change in regards to the things of the spirit. Whether you are a new believer and just learning about the gifts and callings of God, or you are a "seasoned saint" who has been walking with the Lord for quite some time, the fourth section of Stewardship:

9

Managing Your Life Through God's Perfected Pattern is for you in this set time and season of your life.

Elder Burnell Williams, Jr. has written a book that will be a great tool for the body of Christ. I sit and think and it just amazes me at how God loves us so much. He gives us what we need, when we need it even when we don't realize we need it. I have read a lot of books and I have to say that none of them are anything like Stewardship: Managing Your Life Through God's Perfected Pattern. It is no doubt that the man of God has heard from the Lord in writing this book. It is divine inspiration by the Holy Spirit that will touch the heart of men and women around the world. This work of art will leave a lasting legacy on all who read it.

As the saying goes, when you know better you do better. Problem is, a lot of people don't know as much as they think they do. This is especially true when it comes to living your life the way that Christ intended. While reading Stewardship: Managing Your Life Through God's Perfected Pattern, don't just read but open up your heart and mind to actually apply what you read. Life application is how you grow. If you desire to be the best you that you can be, this is the book for you. It changed my life, and it can change yours too.

Nicole Ross

Let's Talk Life: A New Perspective

Table of Contents

<u>Introduction</u>

More than often when we hear the phrase; "good steward" we think of financial responsibility. So let's look at the word steward, in order to gain a clear understanding of its meaning so that we can know how it affects us and our responsibilities towards it.

Webster defines a steward as: (5) one who actively directs affairs – to manage. A good steward is a manager of God's property and affairs because he realizes that God owns everything. Now, you may be thinking, what am I supposed to manage? Why is this even important to me because my life is fine? In either case, we are going to address all of these concerns and give some great principles and examples from the greatest book ever written: the Bible.

Before we get too involved in stewardship, let's look at our Creator and see what He has given us to manage. In the first two chapters of Genesis we find that God not only created the world. (Genesis chapters 1-2) But, he also said that everything was "very good" (Genesis 1:31). You see, God took the time not only to create, but to also thoroughly inspect and do a complete inventory of his creation. Before manager's appeared (Adam) and his wife (Eve), God knew that everything was good and manageable. He already had a plan and pattern established for us to follow.

God gave Adam the privilege of managing in a few areas: His work (Genesis 2:15), taking care of his wife (Genesis 2:24), his family (Genesis 4:1-2), his relationship with God (Genesis 2:16-17) and finally, Adam was to teach his family the ways of God (Genesis 3:2-5).

In this book, we will endeavor to explore how and why we must become better and wiser stewards. Within our families, on our jobs, in our communities, with our finances, with our gifts, and talents, and maintaining our relationship with Christ Jesus. Just to name a few area's that this book will cover.

Section 1: Stewardship of the Steward

"Therefore, brothers, by the mercies of God, I urge you to present your bodies as a living sacrifice, Holy and pleasing to God. This is your spiritual worship"

(Romans 12:1 HCSB)

In the above scripture, the Apostle Paul was addressing the believers in Rome concerning their bodies. This is because consecrating your body is essential for good stewardship! Why, you may wonder? Let's look once again to Paul, "do you not know that your body is the sanctuary of the Holy Spirit who is in you, whom you have from God? You are not your own, for you were bought at a price, therefore glorify God in your body" (1 Corinthians 6:19 HCSB).

Here, Paul lets us know that it is our responsibility to maintain the body that God has loaned to us. It's imperative that you take on and maintain an attitude of management. What I would like you to do is instill this phrase into your mind: *it is loaned to me.*

People more so than ever are joining the health and fitness craze, but, the mentality that we need to grasp and maintain is found in this short verse. "Isn't life more than food and the body more than clothing?"

(Matthew 6:25b HCSB). I'm by no means knocking a healthy lifestyle, nor am I against being presentable. For both of these elements are highly important in order to be a good steward of your body and life.

What I am saying, is to keep your body and life in the best possible condition before God while maintaining an intimate and personal relationship with God first and foremost. After all, it's His temple, and maintaining your life, and body, are your first acts of good stewardship.

<u>YOUR WORK</u>

"But Jesus responded to them, My Father is still working, and I am working also."
(John 5:17 HCSB)

As we discussed in the opening intro: Our Father has given us assignment's to execute but not without an example. From the beginning of creation we have been given the assignment of working. This isn't just a nine to five duty that many dread, but for the good steward it's an opportunity to emulate the Father. By displaying love, instilling hope, and spreading the gospel in your workplace.

Marie worked five days per week for twenty-one years at a paper mill to help support her family since her husband became paralyzed nineteen years prior. She went to work every day with a positive mental attitude because she loved her team and her job

Things were quite difficult, as most can imagine, but Marie trusted God at all times, even when news hit of a departmental lay off. Marie immediately formed a prayer circle with other believers and within a week the news retreated into simply a rumor. During the week of her twenty first anniversary Marie was laid off due to a company merger. After sometime Marie obtained a better job and caught up with some old friends from her old job. They informed her that shortly after she was laid off, the entire company went under.

Now, let's look at what Marie did to become a good steward over her job and how it held an unstable company from going under as long as she was there.

The Bible state's "...don't work only while being watched, in order to please men, but work wholeheartedly, fearing the Lord." (Colossians 3:23b HCSB). As a believer you should outperform unbelievers because you are not working for man only, but for the Lord.

During the best and worst times Marie prayed for her company to prosper and encouraged her teammates to do their best at all times. Look again at what the scripture says, "Whatever you do,

> As a believer you should outperform unbelievers because you are not working for man only, but for the Lord.

do it enthusiastically, as something done for the Lord and not for men knowing that you will receive the reward of an inheritance from the Lord – you serve the Lord Christ." (Colossians 3:23-24 HCSB). Marie's prayers and attitude made her the responsible employee not only for man but for the Lord.

As good stewards on the job we must not view a job as just a paycheck but as an opportunity to share in the Father's duty by causing Heaven to touch and impact the Earth. He work's through and for us as we work the perfected pattern He constructed for us to follow!

I challenge you to step up today as Marie did and become a good steward in your workplace. Maintain your integrity, maintain a positive and productive attitude, pray for every facet and arena of your job, co-workers, supervisor's and display Christ for this will bring God glory and present salvation to the lost and build up the believers around you.

YOUR EDUCATION

"A wise man will listen and increase his learning"
(Proverbs 1:5a HCSB)

In the changing economy, not only are gas prices increasing but the cost of living is on the rise while the average salary is not. In order to increase your income you must increase in educational knowledge and experiential application along with making wise investments.

(1 Samuel 2:3b HCSB) states, "For the Lord is a God of knowledge, and actions are weighed by Him".

Educating yourself enables you to make the best possible decisions in life. Educational stewardship is paramount because it allows you to tap into possibilities and opportunities that you may not have qualified for, or knew anything about.

> You must study as Timothy did in order to properly interpret and teach scripture to others.

Children born into homes where the parents have degrees are more apt to pursue a college education than children with parents who did not attend nor graduated from a technical college or a university.

Educational advancement surpasses just the physical element of life by carrying into the spiritual aspect as well.

(2 Timothy 2:15) instructs us to "study to shew thyself approved unto God, a workman that needeth not to be ashamed, rightly dividing the word of truth (KJV). Here, the Apostle Paul urged the young Pastor Timothy to be diligent in showing God that he was being a good steward of the logos word by studying. This would enable Timothy to be confident, correctly and thoroughly educated, while teaching the gospel and not spreading heresy and embarrassing himself through his incompetence.

When you became a Believer, you were charged and mandated to carry out the Great Commission. So, you must study as Timothy did in order to properly interpret and teach scripture to others. These principles of secular and spiritual education are vital for strength and growth as a well-rounded believer. Pick up a magazine, newspaper, read the company job boards for new opportunities watch the news, but most of all, feast on the word of God.

We will also learn more by active listening to other's than we often realize, so take more time to listen to those around you. There are many valuable lessons to be learned and various ways of learning them. Expand your horizons by deciding today to be a life-long student.

TIME MANAGEMENT

"...making the most of your time"
(Colossians 4:5b HCSB)

"There's not enough time in the day for me." This statement seems to be a popular catchphrase when the fact of the matter is, there has always been twenty four hours within a day. We have just misunderstood the concept of time management by adding more onto our schedules than we should. Productivity has consumed our lives because we have become consumed by the demanding world that we live in. More often than not we don't realize that we may be neglecting family, free-time, church, fitness and other important things. Have you ever been productive and still feel empty even when your goals been met?

To become a good steward of time we should learn from the one who the Bible refers to as the wisest man ever under Christ, King Solomon. In (Ecclesiastes 3:1) Solomon states, "There is an occasion for everything, and a time for every activity under heaven" (HCSB). Meaning: *Balance your time!*

Let's take a look at how this principle works. John Wilkerson, a prominent defense attorney with the Williams & Wilkerson Law Firm, was at the top of his game or so he thought. He is thirty four years old and just made partner with the firm, he is married to Kim and has a wonderful four year old daughter named Summer. They are living the American Dream right? Nice home, new vehicles, friends, money, power and fame. But, let's look a little closer.

For the last ten years John has been so consumed with winning cases trying to make partner that his family barely knows him. Kim, who is a Registered Nurse, has just quit her job to become a full-time homemaker. She cooks, cleans, is involved with church and is currently working on writing children's books. These two have become so consumed with productivity that the family has been neglected, the love and passion they once shared has deteriorated, they once shared one heart but now they barely know one another.

Being overly busy is detrimental to every facet of life while being unproductive will be atrophic to one's life and growth. This is the need of time management. This example is extreme but, this is happening daily.

Let's go back to King Solomon who said, "I know that there is nothing better for them than to rejoice and enjoy the good life. It is also the gift of God whenever anyone eats, drinks and enjoys all of his efforts." (Ecclesiastes 2:12-13 HCSB)

> We have just misunderstood the concept of time management by adding more onto our schedules than we should.

Life and time are precious gifts that are to be used wisely. We can never regain a loss minute so make the most of it. Prioritize your schedule in order to laugh and enjoy the fruits of your labor, enjoy love and live life in a harmonious balance!

<u>YOUR PHYSICAL HEALTH</u>

"Beloved, I wish above all things that thou mayest prosper and be in health, even as thy soul prospers
(3 John 1:2 KJV)

When you think of a healthy lifestyle, what comes to mind? Exercise, nutritious meals, and eight hours of sleep right? Well, these answers are only partially correct, so here's the full truth. In (3 John 1:2) the Apostle John states, "Beloved, I wish above all things that thou mayest prosper and be in health, even as thy soul prospereth". Take notice that John states that the body should prosper simultaneously with the soul. The Apostle Paul reinforced this declaring: "For bodily exercise profiteth little: but godliness is profitable unto all things. Having promise of the life that now is, and of that which is to come" (1 Timothy 4:8 KJV).

Everyone is born with a purpose, and an assignment to fulfill. So we need to be as healthy as possible in order to fulfill them. When our bodies look and feel good, it boosts our self-

33

confidence and moral. Physical health promotes proper blood flow throughout the body, which helps to increase concentration and focus while increasing natural energy. Being healthy also allows your body to heal itself quickly and helps your immune system to fight off illness and unhealthy germs and bacteria. The Lord has given you your body to take care of while walking in your purpose and not to destroy it through negligence and abusive habits.

In order to improve your physical health, you must begin by improving your mental health because some people have a negative self-image. This leads to destructive behavioral patterns throughout life. You must face these faulty mentalities by recognizing your redemptive value and start speaking positive words of affirmation over yourself and surround yourself with godly people who build you up. Remember also, that the truth can be uncomfortable so stick to it because it will pay off.

Physical health can be improved by doing simple things such as walking a mile or two a day consistently in order to work your heart to improve blood pressure and lose weight or maintain a healthy weight. You can also start by drinking eight sixteen ounce bottles of water a day to flush all of the unnecessary toxins out of your body. This maintains your hydration while ensuring good urinary track health.

Even though God is The Healer, if we take the time to exercise and eat properly we can avoid illnesses such as diabetes, high blood pressure, and some strains of cancer just to name a few. The body that we have been given is the only one that we will receive until Christ returns and we receive our glorified bodies. Just like our vehicles, we must maintain our bodies for the best possible performance.

> Everyone is born with a purpose, and an assignment to fulfill, so we need to be as healthy as possible in order to fulfill them.

To maintain, improve, or restore good health, place all of these principles into a harmonious balance daily along with diligence. If you don't know where to start or feel it is too late, repent, then ask God in faith for His strategic wisdom and He will give it. Remember, if you fail to manage your life, your life will manage you!

MONEY MANAGEMENT

"Your life should be free from the love of money."
(Hebrews 13:5a HCSB)

S ociety has truly taken on the mentality that money is the savior of life. It's true that money is necessary to thrive throughout life, but we must manage it and not allow it to manage us. Through commercials and publications, the mainstream media has embedded into our minds the need to have the latest and greatest of everything.

For the most part, people only want the latest and greatest. Where there is nothing wrong with liking and wanting nice things, we cannot become so consumed with living up to the status quo. This type of negligent living can create a financial crisis that will control your life, and you will become enslaved to unmanageable debt.

Watch what Paul tells us about this, "Do not owe anyone anything…" (Romans 13:8a HCSB). Now, in today's society we will always owe at least property taxes, but we should take heed to Paul's instruction before we find ourselves in much unnecessary debt. High credit card bills and interest rates simply because we feel "if I charge this just this one time it won't hurt!" When in fact that one time leads into dozens of times.

So what is the best advice? Begin by repenting to God for not being a good steward over the money He has entrusted to you. Then ask Him for His strategies for your lifestyle. Along with prayer, write out realistic goals for yourself and read them daily. This will help to instill discipline within you, by being a constant reminder of where you want to be. This also helps you to make rational decisions and not impulsive and emotionally based decisions that you will regret later.

As mature believer's we must make our money work for us so we will not have to work so hard for it. Also, some people do not make enough money to support themselves. In this case it's

> As mature believer's we must make our money work for us so we will not have to work so hard for it.

38

imperative to live within your means and even below your means in order to save money to do better. Sacrifice is essential for promotion! Pick up a second job if you must, or go to school and obtain more training in order to increase your income.

For those in debt, start by paying off your smallest debts first while arranging to repay the bigger debts and taking some financial classes. Once we place a proper perspective on finances and our responsibilities on managing it, we become less stressed and free.

Our finances like everything else, is a responsibility God expects us to manage. Make wise decisions with your finances. Learn to go without some of your wants, make wise investments, save for the future and you may even want to take financial counseling but do not allow money nor the benefits of it to manage you!

YOUR THOUGHT LIFE

"For as he thinks within himself, so he is"
(Proverbs 23:7a HCSB).

The thoughts that we think on a momentary basis shape our world, whether for the good or for the bad. For instance: two totally different people can view and perceive the same situation in two different ways and thus responding differently and receiving differing outcomes. The positive thinker sees a challenge as an opportunity to adapt, overcome and ultimately prosper from it. While the negative thinker will become frustrated and complain before avoiding the situation if at all possible. There is also a third person in this scenario: the person who is untrained and uninformed in thought management. This person is unstable and changes with every circumstance.

The Bible teaches us that, "an indecisive man is unstable in all of his ways" (James 1:8 HCSB). James Allen wrote in his book "As a Man Thinketh", "All that a man achieves or fails to

achieve is a direct result of his own thoughts". Dr. Cindy
Trimm also stated "your life moves in

the direction of your thoughts. Thoughts are the ever present
currents that move you either closer or further away from your
best future". I like how Paul addresses it in
(Ephesians 6:17a HCSB) where he states, "take the helmet of
salvation". The reason Paul stated this is because we must
chose to be victorious and think about what you are thinking
about!

The mind is the central battle ground of spiritual warfare!
Often times we are our own enemy because we submit to
negative thoughts. So, rather than being a victim, chose to be a
victor by casting down imaginations, and every high thing that
exalteth itself against the knowledge of God, and bringing into
captivity every thought to the obedience of Christ (2
Corinthians 10:5 KJV). You must chose to believe the truth!

In the book of Numbers we see this principle at work in
its purest form. "Then Caleb quieted the people in the presence
of Moses and said, we must go up and take possession of the
land because we can certainly conquer it"

(Numbers 13:30 HCSB). Now that's the power of positive thinking! Now watch negative thinkers, "but the men who had gone up with him responded, we can't go up against the people because they are stronger than we are"

(Numbers 13:31 HCSB). Now, for the untrained thinker, "to ourselves we seemed like grasshoppers, and we must have seemed the same to them" (Numbers 13:33b HCSB). Caleb thought victorious and later received his prize of entering Kadesh-Barnea, while the negative and untrained thinkers were defeated by themselves and failed to enter with Caleb.

> The thoughts that we think on a momentary basis shape our world, whether for the good or for the bad.

Notice that no one ever spoke to the people, but they *imagined* what others thought of them which caused them to give up.

Now, let's look to King Saul and King David both as additional examples of thought management. In (1 Samuel 17) you will find the epic story of David versus Goliath. The story says that Saul was the acting king of Israel when the Philistines sent their hero Goliath to war against Israel. The future king to reign, David, was on the same battle field as Saul, but perceived the entire situation as an opportunity for God to intervene and save Israel where Saul seen it as a great point of opposition. Thus, David became victorious by slaying the giant while Saul was defeated within himself due to his negative thought process. Victorious living is a choice that is made daily and often times on a momentary basis!

Today, guard your mind by applying the helmet of salvation, cast down all false imaginations by believing what God says about you, your life, family and destiny. Remember to think about what you are thinking about! Think big and live large!

EMOTIONAL MANAGEMENT

"The heart is more deceitful than anything else and desperately sick – who can understand it?"
(Jeremiah 17:9 HCSB)

Conflict resolution teaches "i" before "e" or intelligence over and before emotions. This is important to learn and practice so we won't act or continue to act out of impulse, or feelings which often end in bad calculations. Don't misunderstand me, God gave us emotions but, we are to use our emotions in the proper times and in proper productive ways. Just imagine if every time someone got mad and felt like killing someone and they actually did it. Or, if someone was extremely happy and threw a week-long celebration without going to work and spent all of their money. Emotions have to be managed with intelligence!

Let's look at King David in one of my favorite Psalms, "Why am I so depressed? Why this turmoil within me? Put your hope in God, for I will still praise Him, my Savior and my God" (Psalms 42:11 HCSB). David

45

understood this principle and resolved a conflict before it intensified. A depressing moment can become a chronic illness known as depression. King David noted his feelings and decided to do something about them, he used intelligence and prayer to counter attack his problem. Also notice that David started to encourage himself because he knew that he didn't want to remain in that harmful state of depression.

> Conflict resolution teaches "i" before "e" or intelligence over and before emotions.

Note that our heart will also cause us to say irrational things. "For the mouth speaks from the overflow of the heart" (Matthew 12:34b HCSB). People will often speak out of hurt, anger and confusion and say things like "I hate you" while hurt when in fact they are in love. They are emotionally hurting but won't use intellect until later to discuss the situation and avoid more frustration and pain.

The Bible tells us in (Proverbs 4:23 HCSB) to "guard your heart above all else, for it is the source of life". As stewards, this principle is keen because we must utilize discernment when deciding who we can and cannot share things with and how far to go with the things we share.

To sum this lesson up we'll look to our Savior Jesus, "I, the Lord, examine the mind; I test the heart to give each according to his way. According to what his actions deserve" (Jeremiah 17:10 HCSB). Manage your feelings through the power and gift of logical thinking. To have a clear conscience, the heart and mind must be and remain in alignment. Manage your emotions so your emotions won't manage you.

Section 2: Advancing the Family

"So God created man in His own image; He created Him in the image of God, he created them male and female. God blessed them, and God said to them, "Be fruitful, multiply, fill the Earth, and subdue it. Rule the fish of the sea, the birds of the sky, and every creature that crawls on the earth"
(Genesis 1:28 HCSB).

Notice, that once God commanded Adam and Eve "the newlyweds" to multiply, He told them to subdue the Earth or to obtain knowledge of how the earth could benefit them. This was for them to be able to enter into the next command. Ruling together! In this section of good stewardship, we will obtain knowledge on how to rule together with our families.

As men and women we are both given certain responsibilities in order to manage our families under the perfected pattern of Christ. "And they became one flesh" (Genesis 2:40b HCSB). We must not only learn to become one in the flesh, but also one in purpose and power. The family is the first institution that God created and also the most powerful.

The family is also where the enemy seems to attack the hardest. In this section, we will discuss how the management roles of the husband, wife, and children can work together to live the life that God has ordained for them.

THE HUSBAND

"Husbands, love your wives and don't become bitter against them" (Colossians 3:19 HCSB).

Webster's Dictionary gives two great definitions of a husband: 1. A male partner in marriage. By this direct definition we find that as a man, you are to work together with your wife and not dominate your wife. Before we get to the second meaning of a husband, let's see what Webster says a partner is. One that shares. As husbands we must quickly abandon, the "me, myself and I" mentality that will quickly remove trust, respect and loyalty from our wives. In order to share and become partners we must establish and communicate goals and ideas to and with our wives.

The first role of a husband is to love our wives just as Christ loved the church and gave Himself for her (Ephesians 5:25-26). We are to love her without measure. This type of love is called "Agape" or unconditional love.

> As a husband you are the provider, protector, king, prophet and priest of your home.

The second role of a husband is also found in these scriptures and that is for the husband to have and maintain an intimate personal relationship with Christ and to teach it to his wife. A woman will struggle to submit to a man unless she sees, hears, and knows the God in that man. Even in this she is not submitting to you, but the God in you.

Webster's second definition of a husband is: a manager, steward. In order for us to be managers and stewards we must know and understand what we will have to watch over. The union of marriage is a position of holiness even if you are not saved. For the Bible declares:

"A man who finds a wife finds a good thing and obtains favor from the Lord" (Proverbs 18:22 HCSB).

Marriage is the illustration of the union of the church and Christ. It is also designed to illustrate how the Godhead relates in its separate but unified state (John 17:11). The scriptures state "for the husband is the head of the wife as also Christ is head of the church. He is the Savior of the body" (Ephesians 5:23 HCSB). You are to lead your wife and family into relationship with Christ by example. You are to learn who your wife is, learn the gifts and talents that she possess and by all means, keep her trust!

You have to show her who you are and what direction you are headed in. Utilize both of your skills, talents and strengths to maximize unity and success because the second need of a woman is to know she's valued. By including her in your goals and decision making you show her how valued she is to you.

Remember that as a husband you are the provider, protector, king, prophet and priest of your home. This is the perfect pattern God created for marriage. Know your purpose and follow God's plan in order for your home to prosper. Last but not least, look at the instruction given to husbands in

(Ephesians 5:31), "…a man will leave his father and mother and be joined to his wife, and the two will become one flesh" (HCSB).

Leave your mama and cleave to your wife! When you leave, God can and will weave your home together perfectly. Husbands, when you walk in your true purpose your home will thrive with passion, purpose and power.

THE WIFE

"A capable wife is her husband's crown, but the wife who causes shame is like rottenness in his bones"
(Proverbs 12:4 HCSB).

In the above scripture we find that a good wife is the pride and glory of her husband, while the bad and or untrained wife makes her husband miserable. Let's see what makes a wife the crown of her husband. "It is not good for the man to be alone"

(Genesis 2:18b HCSB). The first purpose of a wife is to be a partner that shares in all of life's affairs with her husband. A wife is a helpmeet, meaning help that is fit for his God given purpose. Women, you are divinely designed to help your husband walk in and fulfill his God given purpose with joy and power.

God took one of his ribs and closed the flesh at that place. Then the Lord God made the rib he had taken from the man into a woman and brought her to the man.

(Genesis 2:21B-22 HCSB).

God could've made the woman independently but he took her from the rib of man so she's intra-dependent. Since the family's direction comes through the believing husband. The purpose of a rib is structure, support, protection and strength. A good wife brings structure and organization into the home. She does this by prioritizing her time, and family activities in order to move the family into the vision, and purpose of her husband. She also provides protection through prayer and encouragement when her husband is down and ready to give up.

She also helps to maintain his God-given vision. The strength and support a good wife provides comes spiritually, emotionally, mentally, socially, physically and if needed, financially.

The good wife's deepest desire should be to learn her husband and his vision in order to support him so they can move

> The purpose of a rib is structure, support, protection and strength.

forward in destiny together as a single unit. This principle is also applied to intimacy.

A wife does not have authority over her own body, but her husband does. Equally, a husband does not have authority over his own body, but his wife does

(1 Corinthians 7:4). Sex should never be out of obligation, but from love. Sex should also never be used as an incentive nor punishment tool (1 Corinthians 7:5). The rib also represents oneness. Marriage is the union of two "man and woman" becoming one unit.

The number one need of your husband is respect. For this reason, the scripture says, "...and the wife is to respect her husband" (Ephesians 5:33 HCSB). When you respect him, he will pour out love, affection and support. The second need of a man is for him to know he's needed by you, so always include him in your decision making and planning even if it's in an area he knows little or nothing about.

You are his helpmeet and he is your visionary. When all this comes together, you help to meet his needs of respect, loyalty, honor, love and stability while he leads you into destiny. You can help to define how great your husband will become by learning and utilizing this pattern for godly success.

When speaking of the famous Proverbs 31 wife, verse 30 states, "charm is deceptive and beauty is fleeting, but a woman who fears the Lord will be praised" (HCSB). Wives, allow your husbands to experience the love God has for him through you.

May your husband always be able to say, "Many women are capable, but you surpass them all" (Proverbs 31:29 HCSB).

YOUR ROMANCE

"Love's flames are fiery flames – the fiercest of all"
(Song of Songs 8:6c HCSB).

This type of love that is fiercely ignited through passion and desire of lovers is called Eros or romantic love. This love is very special because it's a gift from God that's designated to only the married. As we know, Satan has tapped into this awesome experience and tries to kill it in all marriages. Romance is the outward expression of the fiery passion burning within and it is very necessary in keeping a marriage together.

In (Song of Songs 1:2), the woman is talking about her lover when she says, "Oh, that he would kiss me with kisses of his mouth! For your love is more delightful than wine" (HCSB). This is the first step in being romantic; visualizing or imagining your spouse fulfilling you and you fulfilling their intimate desires. Mental passion and stimulation is very keen especially to a woman, because she must be stimulated mentally before the physical element comes into play.

Remember when you first met your spouse and you'd visualize yourselves together and how excited you once were? You'd be excited just being with them even if it were just for a simple walk in the park. That mental stimulation kept both of you excited and wanting more of each other. Something's you can do to start the stimulation process are to send loving texts throughout the day, flowers, and loving emails.

In (Song of Songs 3:7) the man says of his love "How beautiful, my darling, with no imperfection in you" (HCSB). The man here is expressing his desire for his love by expressing his deepest physical attraction and in return the woman expressed hers. "How handsome you are, my love. How delightful!" (Song of Songs 1:16 HCSB) This is essential because the call and return expresses that both parties are ready and willing to set the atmosphere of love and romance while showing their

> Mental passion and stimulation is very keen especially to a woman, because she must be stimulated mentally before the physical element comes into play.

devotion towards one another and confirming that they are still deeply attracted to one another.

Now the atmosphere has been set the anticipation will start to build. Men, you must remember that all women are different just as we are but, there is a universal need for romance. So learn what turns your wife on, as well as how to turn your wife on. Don't assume that what turned her on last year will turn her on today, nor what turned women on in the past will work with your wife.

Romance is imperative to keep passion and pleasure in a marriage. Don't allow your marriage to become routine and dry because marriage and love making is a divine gift that must be valued and cultivated or it will dissipate.

"Come, let's drink deeply of lovemaking until morning. Let's feast on each other's love!" (Proverbs 7:18 HCSB).

Romance can be initiated through romantic dates, meaningful gifts, compliments and your creativity. Keep the pattern and keep the powerful passion! Have fun and keep the love alive! "A loving doe, a graceful fawn – let her breasts always satisfy you; be lost in her love forever" (Proverbs 5:19 HCSB).

<u>YOUR SON'S</u>

"Sons are indeed a heritage from the Lord. Children, are a reward" (Psalms 127:3 HCSB).

C hildren are indeed a blessed reward from the Lord and even the more so when raised in the ways of Christ. Boys are more important than most people realize. Most dads want smart and athletic sons to boost dad's ego. Mothers usually want a smart son that will stay out of trouble, go to college and ultimately become successful while demonstrating a high level of chivalry. Boys are more special than just these aspects of life though.

Boys carry the bloodline of the family in order to establish new generations. As parents, we are to impart Godly characteristics, morals, values and principles into our sons. Instead of speaking negatively about typical boy behaviors we should think of this: inside of every man there is a king and a fool and the one we speak to is the one that will manifest. Bring the king out in your sons so they can become strong stewards in their homes, communities and this nation. King Solomon states:

"the father of a righteous son will rejoice greatly, and one who father's a wise son will delight in him" (Proverbs 23:24 HCSB).

In a world that teaches materialism, fornication, and instant gratification, we should teach our sons that a real man is a man of substance, integrity, wisdom and most of all after God's own heart. This isn't to teach you how to raise your children, but to help you to become good stewards of the son's you've been blessed with. We know that our sons will find their own way. Just as we have, but when a solid foundation is laid and open communication is there, they may stray for a moment but rest assured they will return to the fundamental teachings that you taught them.

Boys need to see and know real men of God because that's who we hope they will become. Men say "I'm a man!" but have no sense of what a real man is to be. We need to get back to the basics of teaching our sons to follow the perfected pattern of success that's found in the word of God. We must teach them to maintain a relationship with God, get an education, career, and then start a family. Give them responsibilities to manage at a young age and hold them accountable for all their actions because every man needs to be responsible and accountable for all their actions in life.

By us modeling what it means to be a good steward, our sons will understand that it's not right nor cool to sleep around with young women leaving emotional scars and often have children with part time or absentee fathers. We need productive sons that will take a stand against Satan and will stay out of gangs, off drugs and out of the prison system.

> Inside of every man there is a king and a fool and the one we speak to is the one that will manifest.

Whether you're a father or mother reading this section and don't know where to begin, start by prayer and the word of God. Find a Godly male role model within your family or your church family. Don't allow the world and media to train your sons in the ways of the world. That will only lead to pain, regrets and uncertainty. By loving them in this way, they'll love you all the more.

YOUR DAUGHTERS

"Thy daughters shall be nursed at thy side"
(Isaiah 60:46 KJV)

G irls are very special because they are the carriers of life so it's imperative that we teach and nurse our daughters to the best of our abilities. Girls learn their expectations of what and how a man should be and how they should be treated by observing their father. Girl's also learn their purpose as a woman and find their identity through their mother.

Both parents are vital and needed to affirm their daughters because of the insecurities which can be picked up in today's society. Society has caused our daughters to place an unhealthy emphasis on superficial things such as their weight, their body shape, their hair, or the size of their breasts. Young women must be taught that true beauty comes from within and is reflected on the outside. They don't need to have premarital sex to obtain, and maintain a relationship. Young women must be taught how to have and maintain an intimate and personal relationship with the Lord Jesus Christ.

They must feel the love of both of their parents and feel the genuine concern for the issues and problems they encounter in life. Even at the early stages of a girl's life, she must reside in an atmosphere of security and experience stability in her life.

Teach your daughter what a wife is so when it's her time to marry she will be confident. The Bible states, "She watches over the activities of her household and is never idle" (Proverbs 31:27 HCSB). Find her true interest in life and support her so she will never feel abandoned and lonely and as a result, go searching for support and love. Today's woman is taught to be strong and independent, but go a step further to teach her how to be wise. For wisdom is necessary in order for a woman to reign as a queen.

A certain level of independence is good while growing and living as a single woman but she cannot be independent as a married woman so fathers should continue to provide for and protect their daughters until marriage. This will teach her how to trust her husband and show her what the leadership role of a man is and how she is to be his helpmeet "help that is fit" throughout their life.

Teach your daughter how to overcome her shortcomings and mistakes in life by sharing your own personal testimonies with her. Never leave her alone to fight battles if you can help it. She will be a mother one day and will pass down the principles and values you share and teach. Become one with her spiritually, emotionally, mentally, physically and through effective communication. By being

> Both parents are vital and needed to affirm their daughters because of the insecurities which can be picked up in today's society.

a good steward of her, she will become a good steward of her own family and of her own life one day.

THE COLLECTIVE FAMILY

"As for me and my family, we will worship the Lord"
(Joshua 24:15b HCSB)

.

Each individual has unique needs, so when the family joins together in unison there are also management principles that we should apply. The first principle is the love and unity of the family. Parents should always stick together in agreement with each other on decisions that are made and on rules to be enforced. This will promote respect, enforce obedience and demonstrate the power of unity even if you, as parents, don't always agree. As adults you should always talk about your differences in private.

The family as a whole must be taught to demonstrate unity because unity is the demonstration of the power of love. The enemy loves to attack the home front so where there's unity there's strength and power. Never down one another but always strive to complement and enhance one another because this produces confidence and a sense of self-worth. Anytime children feel unloved and lonely they will search for acceptance elsewhere.

Stay current on technology, music, popular topics and the interests of your children. They need your support and to know that you're interested in them. Establish times for family dinners and outings, family prayer and Bible study times. These practices are imperative! Ask questions about what your family is learning every week in school and church.

This will also alert everyone to the callings, gifting's and talents in each other. Have your son's open doors for their mother and sisters to teach them how to treat women. Likewise for daughters to support and uphold their brothers and father so that they will know how to respect and esteem men. Respect is the number one need of men, as security is the first need of a woman.

Share your plans, visions, and projects with the family and invite them to share their ideas. When it's time for discipline allow them to tell you what they did wrong and talk about how to correct the problem and prevent further problems. This promotes responsibility and accountability throughout their lives. As we know every family is different and has unique needs but we all have the same responsibilities to become good stewards in and over our home. A strong home makes for a strong community, state, nation and world. Remember one day your family may have to become stewards over you.

Parents, "teach a youth about the way he should go; even when he is old he will not depart from it" (Proverbs 22:6 HCSB). Likewise, the Bible instructs children on how to treat their parents, "honor your father and mother – which is the first commandment with a promise – that it may go well with you and that you may have a long life in the land" (Ephesians 6:2-3 HCSB).

> The family as a whole must be taught to demonstrate unity because unity is the demonstration of the power of love.

Remember, at the end of the day, family is all you have and the most valuable asset you have. Invest into your family members and I promise the dividends will be tremendous!

<u>YOUR LEGACY</u>

"Grandchildren are the crown of the elderly"
(Proverbs 17:6a HCSB).

More often than not children are absolutely in love with their grandparent's. This is because of the unlimited love and attention they receive. Take notice also that grandparents also discipline sternly and pass on their personal values while enforcing the values and ethics they taught you. Passing on a legacy is extremely important because God holds us responsible to lay a solid foundation for the third and fourth generations. I believe that King Solomon wrote (Proverbs 17:6) because he was excited about seeing his children and the children of others walk in and practice the ways of God that were passed down to them.

The family values we instill into our children are more than just for them to become responsible, ethical, and productive citizens, but also because your legacy is being built. It's August of 2011 and I can still remember my grandfather in his bedroom kneeling beside his bed praying. He died in the early 1990s but, those memories taught me the importance of having a solid prayer life and I have passed that on to my daughter, because we pray together.

Children also love and dream about being financially stable like their grandparents because grandparents are usually the ones spoiling them with gifts. This imprints everlasting memories and raises standards to be followed by the next generation. As parents, I feel we should share the past struggles and traditions of our parents and grandparents with our children. So they will have and take pride in the family name and have a

> Passing on a legacy is extremely important because God holds us responsible to lay a solid foundation for the third and fourth generations.

strong sense of purpose in life. As an African American male I feel proud of my heritage knowing where my family has come from. Therefore, I have set a standard of excellence for my daughter to teach her children's children.

In biblical times godliness was handed down from generation to generation as were trades and positions such as kingship. A great example of this is when the Reubenites,

Gadites and half of the tribe of Manasseh built a large and impressive altar by the Jordan River in the Promised Land of Canaan. They did this to pass the legacy of worship to the true and living God of the world (Joshua 22:26-31).

You can also set up trust funds for your children in order for them to have a jump start in life and not start off struggling as so many do. No matter how old children get, they'll never outgrow your love. Let's take pride and joy in building a generational legacy. It's an awesome privilege of stewardship.

Section 3: Advanced Leadership

"Obey your leaders and submit to them, for they keep watch over your souls as those who will give an account, so that they can do this with joy and not with grief, for that would be unprofitable for you" (Hebrews 13:17 HCSB)

O nce we came into the body of Christ we all became leaders and for some you were leaders before your conversion, but as leaders we must be the first to fully submit to higher leadership such as pastors, church officials, and other governing authority figures. In life we all have to answer to some form of higher authority at one point or another. We all know and were taught that leaders lead but the greatest leader of all, Jesus Christ, came to serve.

From washing feet, healing, raising the dead, being beaten, crucified and rising from the dead, Jesus was constantly serving. When I was in the Army I often heard the phrase "lead by example". This is the basic and most important part of leadership. Remember, leadership is a position and not a title. You don't have to be a CEO, President, Boss, Pastor, or anything else in order to lead. Most good leaders are the laymen who hold no position at all, but they have influence. By submitting and serving you gain the most influence because you show that you genuinely care and are concerned about people and their individual needs.

In this section we will discuss leadership principles in various areas and discover how to become good stewards over the position God has entrusted us with. Let's go higher together my friend.

THE CHURCH

"Christ is the Head of the church"
(Ephesians 5:23a HCSB).

The church is a joint body of believers that join together collectively to meet with and experience God. While worshipping God in a corporate setting and fellowshipping, we also help to strengthen one another. With this comes the responsibility of stewardship, since God gave us this awesome privilege to manage His stuff. As believers we should not only attend a church, but become involved within the body. By becoming active we become a part of something much greater than ourselves once we have the perspective of a good steward.

Becoming actively involved helps in our sanctification because we have people that will hold us accountable for our walk, faith and ministry.

The church is a great place to become a part of other's lives on new levels. By sharing our time in getting to know people we begin to share our testimonies, which often will open doors for healing and deliverance. This goes not only for others but for yourself as well. A lot of times sharing our issues helps us to gain deliverance. The enemy loves to make us feel alienated as if we are the only one going through our hardships but sharing our testimony is a great way of healing and showing loving concern for others who are in similar situations.

Another great benefit is to network. Within the local body you will find all sorts of people with different outlooks, backgrounds and professions. If you cannot use their area of expertise, you will definitely have resources to pass on to others. As workmen for God you will also automatically start to flow in blessings.

Now realize all blessings aren't money nor material gain. Some blessings will be friendships, spiritual gifts, health, maturity, etc. I love Dr. Creflo Dollar's definition of the blessing: The supernatural empowerment to succeed in every area of life. Taking a stand in church is taking a stand in your local community and your impact will be invaluable.

You don't have to preach, sing, usher, nor be a deacon or anything with a title. You can help park cars, paint, cook, clean or many other things based on the needs of the ministry. The most important thing is to carry out the Great Commission and represent the Kingdom well. Jesus told His disciples "Go, therefore, and make disciples of all nations, baptizing them in the name of the Father and the Son and the Holy Spirit, teaching them to observe everything I command you." (Matthew 28:19-20a HCSB).

> Becoming actively involved helps in our sanctification because we have people that will hold us accountable for our walk, faith and ministry.

This also matures and cultivates your gifts, talents and calling while enforcing godly values in your home and community. Once you join the body you are a part of the body so become a great asset and not just another name on the church attendance roll. God blesses us for the purpose of blessing others.

YOUR COMMUNITY

"The community assembled as one body before the Lord"
(Judges 20:1b HCSB).

We all know that our entire community may not be saved, nor even know and associate with one another. As stewards of the gospel we have civil responsibilities in and for our communities. Most places have a community watch program in effect, but, I'm talking about the deeper issues such as interceding on behalf of your community. Pray that God's hand is upon your local government officials and voting in order for your voice to be heard. The decisions you make will not only affect your future but also that of your children.

You can pray and pray, but as James tells us, "In the same way faith, if it doesn't have works, is dead by itself" (James 2:17 HCSB).

While involved within your local church you can find less fortunate families and help them out. This could turn their lives around forever. Teach your children about giving back to the community, because your community is a part of you. I once heard an old African proverb that says, "It takes a village to raise a child". This is true because as parents we lay the foundation for our children's lives. There are also other people that will impact, shape and influence our children into who

> The only way for our nation to change is for our communities to change.

they will ultimately want to become. Get out and get to know the parents and friends of your children because you don't want your child to learn and become engaged in the wrong things.

As believers we also have the responsibility to be the light of the world and the salt of the earth

(Matthew 5:13-16). Make time to be involved in charities because this promotes pride, friendships, growth and responsibility as well as being great for networking. By becoming good stewards in your communities you make an impact that you can't begin to imagine. Sometimes it takes only one person to start building the momentum and motivation for change. The only way for our nation to change is for our communities to change.

Go to a school and read to children, support the girl scouts, attend a neighborhood car wash and watch the happiness in the faces of people. I promise it will become contagious! Yes, we as good stewards are our brother's keeper. Be blessed in all of your new endeavors.

YOUR FRIENDSHIPS

"A friend loves at all times, and a brother is born for a difficult time" (Proverbs 17:17 HCSB).

True friends are very hard to find these days, as we know, so these relationships must be cherished and valued. I believe true friends are gifts that God places in our lives to help us along the way. One of the most important aspects of friendship is honesty. A friend must keep it real at any and all costs. Honesty will more often than not promote loyalty among you. As we already know, love is the foundation and prerequisite for successful friendships. While no two people are exactly alike we must agree to disagree. After all, if people were exactly alike someone will be unnecessary in the relationship.

While in the Army I was assigned to what is called a battle buddy. This person is not only a friend but a true lifeline. Battle buddies do almost everything together because if something happens to one of them, the other is there to go to battle with and for him. This is an awesome relationship that takes place from basic training and sometimes will last an entire lifetime. This Army value is the perfect example of the opening scripture. When you enter into friendships you must be willing to truly be there for the person and allow them to be there for you. It's not a give me, give me type of thing, but a give and take bond. So, you must communicate boundaries and

> Love is the foundation and prerequisite for successful friendships.

not assume your boundaries are common sense nor alike.

The perfect example of this is the relationship of King David and Jonathan. "Jonathan committed himself to David, and loved him as much as he loved himself"

(1 Samuel 18:1 HCSB). Jonathan not only committed himself to be David's friend but also committed himself to the relationship of the two. These were true battle buddies because Jonathan was almost killed trying to protect his friend's life (1 Samuel 20:32-42).

I truly urge you to hold on to your true friends and if you don't have a close friend remember: to be a friend, show yourself to be friendly (Proverbs 18:24a). Also don't invest time in vain relationships once you see there's no progression between you. Sometimes people are in your life for a season and you can't be afraid to let them go. Everyone isn't meant to last a lifetime! Pray with and for one another, laugh together, cry together and enjoy one another.

FELLOWSHIPPING

"But if we walk in the light as He Himself is in the light, we have fellowship with one another" (1 John 17a HCSB).

The New Unger's Bible Dictionary defines fellowship as: Companionship, a relationship in which parties hold something in common. We all have friends and family but we don't always have time or feel the need for fellowship. I used to be one of the one's in church that praise, worship, eat of the word and I'm the first out the door headed to my vehicle. Because of my lack of fellowship, when I faced problems I had no spiritual support system. Of course, I had my pastor, but I had no spiritual brothers and sisters. I was walking in the spirit of excellence but often was not victorious.

Fellowshipping is like your white blood cells, when something foreign enters the body a call is sent out and all the white blood cells join together in power and authority and counter attack the foreign agent producing victory. Fellowshipping helps in the sanctification process because you are held accountable for your actions. Look at James on this point, "Therefore, confess your sins to one another and pray for one another so that you may be healed. The intense prayer of the righteous is very powerful"

(James 5:16 HCSB).

Fellowshipping is also a tool of concern that expresses love, concern and hope. (Romans 15:12) emphasizes that the strong person is to bear the problems and concerns of the weaker individual. This is awesome because we are responsible to uplift one another and to hold one another accountable for growth. Also notice in (Acts 2:1) that the Apostles were joined together in fellowship when they were all filled with the Holy Spirit on the Day of Pentecost.

Fellowship invokes the presence and power of God to show up and be displayed (Matthew 18:20). Fellowship is so important to God that Christ even prayed for His people to fellowship with one another

> Fellowshipping is also a tool of concern that expresses love, concern and hope.

(John 17:21). By walking in the unity of fellowship you also render and receive great service. You'll have the opportunity to bless those brothers and sisters in financial need or receive if you're in direct need. see (Romans 12:13)

In tough economic times, networking is essential because in a lot of cases it's not what you know but who you know. The need for stewardship in this arena of life is paramount because fellowship is very powerful and important but is often neglected. (John 15:4-5) enforces the constant need of fellowship of the believer with our Savior and Father. Without fellowship with Him we are fruitless, defeated,

non-productive to the Kingdom and are outside of His perfected pattern and plan that's been set forth.

In (John 15:15b) Jesus calls us His friends because of our fellowship and intimacy with Him. Fellowship in the spiritual and natural realm is imperative for you and the people around you. Become more social and watch new doors open in your life.

YOUR INTEGRITY

"Set an example of good works yourself, with integrity and dignity in your teaching. Your message is to be sound beyond reproach, so that the opponent will be ashamed, having nothing bad to say about us" (Titus 2:7b-8 HCSB).

The definition of integrity has various meanings to different people. Maybe that's why the hearts, minds and lifestyles of many are not with God's pattern for success. Webster defines it as follows: firm adherence to a code of especially moral or artistic values – incorruptibility. Also the Hebrew word Tummah is translated into integrity or innocence. Integrity is to be a vital part of the believer's physical life. As well as their spiritual life, in order to maintain a clear conscious before God. Integrity will assist you so you will not misrepresent and mishandle the word and power of God (Acts 24:16).

There's also another definition which is the most common but most overlooked: honesty. I once heard a story that says: In the beginning of time truth and lie were best friends. They did everything together. As time went on, lie became jealous of truth because truth was better at everything and succeeded in everything.

So, lie became envious and began to plot on truth in an effort to destroy him. Lie told truth "Let's have a race. We'll swim from the dock of this lake to the billow and around it and back." Truth agreed and they both got undressed and laid their clothes on the dock. On the count of three they both jumped in and began to swim. Truth lead the way and took the lead in the race instantly.

By the time truth went around the billow he saw lie jumped out of the lake and put on his clothes. He did this because truth is rich and has nicer clothes because he was important and lie is poor and meager. So lie took off running with truth chasing him. Truth is still chasing him to this very day. The moral of the story is, whenever you see a well-dressed lie, remember the naked truth is right behind him!

This story is a fable but has a real message to it. As believers we possess the Spirit of Truth that we are mandated to walk in on a daily basis (John 16:13-14). As we discussed in the

Stewardship of the Steward introduction, we are not our own once we have undergone the new birth process. Integrity must be managed on a consistent basis so that we will not mishandle the word of God.

"But an hour is coming, and now is here, when the true worshippers will worship the Father in Spirit and truth. Yes, the Father wants such people to worship Him. God is Spirit, and those who worship Him must worship in Spirit and truth" (John 4:23-24 HCSB).

To truly worship and serve God we must operate in integrity and not compromise at all in any avenue or arena of life. I strongly encourage you today to not compromise, maintain your innocence and to be honest in all

> Integrity is to be a vital part of the believer's physical life and also their spiritual life in order to maintain a clear conscious before God and not to misrepresent and mishandle the word and power of God.

you say, do and even think. "But let your communication be yea, yea; nay, nay: for whatsoever is more than these cometh of evil" (Matthew 5:37 KJV).

My prayer is that you will walk in victory and the spirit of excellence from this day forward while maintaining the highest level of integrity possible. I love you and God does too.

RIGHT LEGAL STANDING

"Everyone must submit to the governing authorities, for there is no authority except from God, and those that exist are instituted by God. So then, the one who resists the authority is opposing God's command, and those who oppose it will bring judgment on themselves"
(Romans 13:1-2 HCSB).

Not only as Believers, but as people we all have the moral and civil duty to keep and abide by the laws of the land. By observing and obeying the laws we not only maintain a clear conscience before God, but also man. Most of the civil laws were based on biblical principles, also by keeping the law we live above reproach and maintain a clear conscience in every arena of life. There are also blessings that follow us remaining in obedience to the law.

Today there are a tremendous amount of believer's that are incarcerated around the world. This is because we can and will yield to various temptations. Seeing a temptation is not a sin, but contemplating enough that you act upon that temptation is a sin. Once a person is convicted in the court of law for violating a law the judge will impose a sentence such as probation, jail or prison. Now for the next ten years you have to pay for the sin that only lasted a matter of minutes.

This is also what happened in the Garden of Eden (Genesis 3:1-7). Thousands of years later we are still paying the price for the sins that were committed because we are born into sin and we have to endure sickness, stress, and death. We were never meant to deal with these things (Genesis 3:17-19).

There are millions of people in the U.S. that are in the prison system. We can drop these numbers by taking five to ten minutes to think things through before we act and respond to life's choices. In the spiritual realm, some believe that you can do what you want and at the end of the day say "Lord forgive me" and the next day do it all over again without consequence. True repentance is for unintentional sins and sins that you didn't think through. To just use grace as a crutch is simply lawlessness that will be punished.

My definition of true repentance is an inward change that produces outward results. When our mind changes our actions change. Sin separates us from Christ (Isaiah 59:21) on all

levels, so we must not only look at the temptation, but consider the outcome, count the total cost. Jesus said "I have come that they may have life and have it in abundance"
(John 10:10b HCSB).

I encourage you my friend to obey the laws of man and most importantly the perfect laws of our Lord and Savior Jesus Christ.

"For rulers are not a terror to good conduct, but too bad. Do you want to be unafraid of the authority? Do good and you will have its approval."

> By observing and obeying the laws, we not only maintain a clear conscience before God but also man.

(Romans 13:3 HCSB)

To have the abundant life and remain from under the wrath of the law, resist your evil temptations even if you have to run away from them.

YOUR VISION

"Write down this vision, clearly inscribe it on tablets so one may easily read it" (Habakkuk 2:2 HCSB).

C hazon is the Hebrew translation of the word vision which means a mental sight, a revelation, an oracle and a prophecy. A vision is a plan of purpose given to man from God to specifically direct and guide a leader and his people into destiny. Where this is my personal revelation, I believe it's very accurate. Every person born is born with and for a purpose. For some people, their purpose is revealed to them because they seek it or have great talents. Where others will live their entire lives wondering why they were put here on the Earth.

I believe this is why King Solomon wrote "where there is no vision, the people perish"

(Proverbs 29:18a KJV).

As leaders and stewards of the gospel, we have a vision to advance the Kingdom in its fullness one life at a time. Where no two people have the same exact vision, plan, purpose or revelation, we all are responsible to manage what God has directed us to do. When you receive your vision the word says that you are to write it down. By writing the vision it becomes plain to use and you can begin to come into complete agreement with it. This also enables you to pray on the vision and begin to write smaller goals to accomplish the vision and to gather people and resources.

It also give you momentum in spiritual, mental, financial, emotional and social growth. As well as keeping you focused and in tune with God and His plan and timing for your life.

The second part of the scripture instructs and advises that it must be accessible for others to see and understand. As leaders the anointing that's on your life gives you Kingdom influence. Which means people must buy into you before they

> A vision is a plan of purpose given to man from God to specifically direct and guide a leader and his people into destiny.

buy into your vision. A vision happens when God takes His

thoughts and plans, and infuses them into your spirit in order for you to live in purpose. He lays out his plan and gives it to you and your ministry to rely on Him to direct and complete. This is where good stewardship comes in. It's His pattern that must be carried out His way and on His timeline.

As the visionary you are to recruit and utilize people with the proper gifts, talents, and anointing's for the particular assignments that the Holy Spirit directed you to give. These people will also share the same passion and excitement as you. The people may also have smaller visions and plans that God will give them to incorporate into their assignments. Use discernment and allow room for some creativity as the Spirit leads.

"For the vision is yet for the appointed time, it testifies about the end and will not lie. Though it delays, wait for it, since it will certainly come and not be late" (Habakkuk 2:3 HCSB).

Sometimes God will reveal a vision in order to start his preparation process in you and other's around you but don't become discouraged, be encouraged! Pray to find out when the vision is to start and take place. As a child I had visions and prophesies of me being a great preacher that even carried into my adult life. With this vision came years of processing preparing me before I could step into destiny. I was shown the vision years in advance to help me to understand the processing period that I had to undergo and not lose hope.

Vision is a spiritual destination set by God for his leader to see, and lead people under His influence into. Remember that vision is a place of rest that satisfies the Lord and rewards others where imagination is self-gratifying and self-centered.

Write your vision for direction and motivation not only for others but also for yourself. Be a good steward over the vision God has given you.

<u>Section 4: Spiritual Stewardship</u>

"Blessed be the God and Father of our Lord Jesus Christ, who hath blessed us with all Spiritual blessings in heavenly places in Christ" (Ephesians 1:3 KJV).

P neumatikos is the Greek word for 'spiritual' that means by the assistance of the Holy Spirit. In becoming a good steward over every spiritual blessing that God has given to us, we must be aware that they are entrusted to us by God. For his purposes as the Holy Spirit directs. As soon as we allow the pride of the eyes, lust of the flesh, and pride of one's lifestyle to kick into play, we will face a dramatic consequence. Let's take a look at king Nebuchadnezzar.

"At the end of twelve months, as he was walking on the roof of the royal palace in Babylon the king exclaimed, "is this not Babylon the Great that I have built by my vast power to be a royal residence and to display my majestic glory?" While the words were still in the king's mouth, a voice came from

Heaven: "King Nebuchadnezzar, to you it is declared that the kingdom has departed from you" (Daniel 4:29-31 HCSB).

Notice in (Daniel 3:29) King Nebuchadnezzar had an experience with God and not only issued decrees for his kingdom to worship God, but he also became a servant of God before pride consumed him.

In this section you will discover and learn or become refreshed in the following areas: ministering, forgiveness, intercession, the anointing and much more. I encourage you to become and remain all God has called you to be with uncompromising power, authority, wisdom, understanding and humility. I pray this will enhance, enlighten and inspire you in your walk with Christ.

YOUR SPIRITUAL GIFTS

"A manifestation of the Spirit is given to each person to produce what is beneficial" (1 Corinthians 12:7 HCSB).

S piritual gifts must be managed and maintained according to God's pattern for them to be most effective. God gives gifts not for selfish desires but for the edification of the body of Christ. For this reason, God has distributed a measure of faith to each and every believer according to their individual capacities. "Spiritual gifts" can be defined as supernatural gifts of empowerment entrusted to a believer for the advancement of the Kingdom of God. Every believer is given a spiritual gift once they have received the Holy Spirit.

"A demonstration of the Spirit is given to each person to produce what is beneficial" (1 Corinthians 12:7 HCSB).

The need of good stewardship is because you are commissioned to build the Kingdom through the power and direction of the Spirit. There are three types of gifts that are given and entrusted to Believers: motivational, manifestation

111

and ministry (1 Corinthians 12:4-7). To effectively and efficiently manage your gifts you must first understand the gifts. Under each category of gift, I will list an example for you to identify with and its purpose.

- Ministry: prophets (proclaim God's will, disclose future events) and teachers (clarify the truth, validate information). There are also

- Motivational gifts: exhorting (stimulate faith, promote growth), serving (meet needs, free others).

- Manifestation: Miracles (supernatural deeds, activate faith), healing (to include mind, body, emotions, and families).

These were just a few examples. If you do not know your gift, start by prayer. Ask God for clarity and concentrate on the needs of others (Ephesians 4:12-13). Distinguish the true characteristics and misuses of each gift. Along with this you must stay before God's face in constant prayer, fellowship, study and obedience. Just as there are variations of gifts there are also various levels of these gifts. As you begin to grow and mature in Christ and the needs of the body of Christ grows, so will your gifts begin to mature in power.

I encourage you to "study to show yourself approved as a workman that's not ashamed" (2 Timothy 2:15) and also sit under mature and anointed mentors with the same passion and gifts. This will encourage, develop and also enhance you until you're all that you can be for the Kingdom. This is a great stewardship responsibility that cannot be

> Spiritual gifts must be managed and maintained according to God's pattern for them to be most effective.

neglected in anyway. "For the Kingdom of God is not in talk but in power" (1 Corinthians 5:20 HCSB).

I encourage you my friend to continue to walk in God's gifting of power and authority. Be blessed in the mighty and holy name of Jesus!

YOUR DELIVERANCE

"Behold, I stand at the door, and knock: if any man hear my voice, and open the door, I will come in to Him, and will sup with him, and he with me" (Revelation 3:20 KJV).

Aphesis is the Greek translation for deliverance which means "freedom, pardon, forgiveness, liberty, and remission". Initially, deliverance is obtained at and through salvation where one is freed from the power of sin. The believer is pardoned or forgiven of all past sins and prodigal living, and is positioned into the perfect liberty of the Holy Spirit. This is the greatest level of deliverance that one can ever receive and how awesome it is!

As believers grow and mature in the Lord they will undergo levels of specific deliverance. This will come through the Holy Spirit revealing you to yourself, as you confess your shortcomings and sins to yourself, God and even spirit-filled believers. These shortcomings that are in your life can range from addictions, lying, fornication, to slothfulness, self-destructive mentalities, or deep rooted hurt from your past just to name a few. Deliverance is the process of which the Holy Spirit reveals these things to you and sanctifies you for further Kingdom service.

Sanctification is a threefold process and is progressive throughout our lives. These steps are as follows:

- Positional – (1 Corinthians 1:2, Hebrew 10:10, Jude 1, Titus 3:5, and 1 John 3:9) You are sanctified in Christ by His redemptive work on the cross for your sins.

- Progressive – (Philippians 2:12, Hebrews 9:14, Psalms 79:9, and 1 Peter 1:16) The Holy Spirit is constantly working within you cleansing and empowering you until death or Christ's return.

- Consumational – (2 Timothy 1:12, Philippians 3: 21, and 1 Corinthians 15:23, 49) Your sanctification will be complete upon Christ's return and you receive your glorified body.

As believers grow and mature in the Lord they will undergo levels of specific deliverance.

As long as you're in the flesh and striving in the spirit of excellence, you will continue the sanctification process in order to be like Christ.

In order to maintain the deliverance that you've received and will receive, you must know there's no good thing in the flesh, and you need the help of the Holy Spirit to live a holy life. You must know your weakness and set boundaries and limitations for yourself. Have mature accountability partners who you trust for spiritual and natural support (James 5:16).

Know that the enemy is patient and will wait for an opportune time to tempt you (John 10:10, Matthew 12: 43-45). Satan's job is to tempt you and your job is to recognize Him, resist Him, and release the word of God over yourself because faith and strength comes through the word! James tells us that we are only driven away and enticed by our own evil desires because of the issues lying within our hearts that want to be fulfilled (James 1: 14-15, 4:7).

Know that God will make a way of escape for you and you won't be tempted above what you can handle

(1 Corinthians 10:13). Stay rooted and grounded in your local body for strength and support. If you fall don't stay down! Get up! See yourself as God sees you! Release words of affirmation over yourself if need be. Pray and pray in the Spirit to edify yourself and receive God's strategies for your life and situation.

Be aggressive about maintaining your deliverance and walking in newness of life or on a high level. Keep closed doors closed in your life. Lastly, be prepared to stand alone. This is because God sanctified us according to our function and purpose within the body (James 4:17). Some may not understand you and will tell you "it don't take all that". Live according to your convictions and not man-made standards.

I encourage you that no matter where you are within your walk with the Lord to lean upon the Lord daily, make Him your stronghold. You're in spiritual warfare for your soul. By utilizing this pattern for success you will walk in the freedom of the Holy Spirit. Remember: get delivered and stay delivered!

YOUR ANOINTING

"Their anointing will serve to inaugurate a permanent priesthood for them throughout their generations"
(Exodus 40:15b HCSB).

My definition of the anointing is, a divine empowerment given to a believer to carry out their assignments and operate effectively in their gifts and calling.

A great example of this is "As a result, they would carry the sick out into the streets and lay them on beds and pallets so that when Peter came by, at least his shadow might fall on some of them. In addition, a multitude came together from the towns surrounding Jerusalem, bringing sick people and those who were tormented by unclean spirits, and they were all healed" (Acts 5:15-16 HCSB). There's no surprise nor question that the Apostle Peter was walking in a great anointing.

This empowerment is often flaunted by many believers because of their lack of good stewardship. The anointing on your life must be maintained with a Godly attitude, obedience, and self-control. The anointing that is entrusted to you is not to glorify your ministry, but for your ministry to glorify God by destroying the yokes of bondage on God's people (Isaiah 10:27).

Elisha the predecessor of Elijah knew that he had a great work to do in building the faith, hope and community of Israel. When the time for his mentor to depart had come he asked for a double portion of his anointing

(2 Kings 2:9b) of which he received. As you continue to read the story, you will see that immediately Elisha stepped into his ministry and had to lead, advise and help his people. The anointing he asked for was to help him to lead an entire nation to their father. With a great calling comes a great responsibility.

As an anointed steward you must be very careful not to fall into the, me, myself and I mentality that will quickly lead you into grave danger and destruction. Also notice that during Elisha's first miracle (v. 19-22) with the bad water, he didn't act on his own accord and power, but he humbled himself to hear from God for direct instructions that lead into a generational miracle. This is what I call "the Greater Blessing". This blessing is one that exceeds human standards, expectations and powers because it's designed to flow into other's not just you. Elisha may have been able to cure the water through his anointing, but he heard from God first. Why have good water for a day or week, when God will give a generational overflow?

> The anointing is, a divine empowerment given to a believer to carry out their assignments and operate effectively in their gifts and calling.

Your anointing carries great responsibilities and burdens. As you know, it's easy to become self-consumed and also influenced by popularity and people, so stay before God for Him to keep you humble. You may be anointed to heal, but a person may be in a season where God has placed them for a reason and you are not to interfere because if they come out prematurely it will hurt them in the long run. Remember, your anointing is for and from God not to glorify and appease man.

Don't ever think or feel that you are less anointed by looking at others, we are partnered with God in different ways at different times to build the Kingdom. Never become so consumed in Kingdom work that you forget about the King!

YOUR CALLING

"I, therefore, the prisoner in the Lord, urge you to walk worthy of the calling you have received with all humility and gentleness, with patience, accepting one another in love, diligently keeping the unity of the Spirit with the peace that binds us"(Ephesians 4:1-3 HCSB).

Walking worthy of your calling is imperative for the maximum impact for the Kingdom. This principle is an essential in good stewardship that many believers are forsaking. There are men and women of God that have become so complacent in their walk and ministry that they simply go through the motions. They no longer pray like they should. They no longer study and spend intimate time with the Savior because they feel like they have it all together because they have been doing it so long.

Also there's a tragic phenomenon going on in many churches of people operating in a mode of falsetto. Falsetto is defined as: An artificially produced singing voice that overlaps and extends above the range of the full voice. What's happening is people are operating in an artificial state that cannot and will not last. Because you are called to preach does not mean that you are to be promoted or promote yourself to a Pastor's position. If you are called to teach that does not mean you should become a prophet.

When you act outside of your calling you stand in disobedience and cause chaos within the body". But, everything must be done decently and in order"

(1 Corinthians 14:40 HCSB).

To walk worthy means to maintain a clear conscience before both God and man. Every believer needs to obtain a clear understanding of who they are in Christ and their purpose within the kingdom. Seek God's face to learn their direct area of operation or spiritual niche in the church. You must always seek to learn more and to grow into maturity in Christ (2 Timothy 2:15). A teacher, for example, may be called but his or her area of operation may be in jails, prisons and communities. Where another teacher's area of operations may be with young adults and specialized classes in the church.

When these two operate within their scope of ministry, God shows up and changes lives, but when they go into falsetto mode then things crumble. God has not only called you, but has chosen you for a special work in building the Kingdom. While some operations may seem and look more glorious than others, remember that we are many parts but still there is only one body (1 Corinthians 12:12-31 HCSB).

Walk worthy of your calling by learning and becoming all that God has ordained for you to become and do it to the best of your ability with a positive and enthusiastic attitude. "God has put the body together, giving greater honor to the less honorable, so that there would be no division in the body, but that the members would have the same concern for each other" (1 Corinthians 12:24b-25 HCSB).

> Walking worthy of your calling is imperative for the maximum impact for the Kingdom.

Today I speak new life and encouragement into you and your ministry. Be all you can be in the army of the Lord!

YOUR TALENTS

"A gift opens doors for a man and brings him before the great"
(Proverbs 18:16 HCSB).

As a young boy, my friend Ken had the natural ability to go into his mother's kitchen and turn a few simple items into a lavish dish. As Ken grew older, his natural abilities started maturing and naturally he had the passion to become a chef. At the age of nineteen, Ken's culinary talent led him to become part owner of a fantastic four star Italian restaurant. His talents have led him to meet and exceed the skills of chefs that have attended a culinary institute.

When I asked him how he became so creative, his reply was that he was constantly reading about new culinary and hospitality trends. Watching special television programs and he said that he's truly motivated by God to become the very best chef that he can become.

Today Ken has faced many struggles, to include going to prison. Even during the toughest of times he wrote recipes and subscribed to magazines to maintain his momentum to become a world class chef. With his tenacious attitude and passionate drive, I believe he will one day become a world renowned chef. You may have the same talent as Ken, or a totally different talent altogether, but God has given every person a special talent that needs to be found, cultivated and maintained. The earlier you find, develop, and utilize your talents, the longer you have to use them.

> The earlier you find, develop, and utilize your talents, the longer you have to use them.

It is also important to know that talents differ from gifts. Talents are natural abilities that are used in the physical, where gifts are spiritual endowments that have a physical manifestation. Some people find their talents early in life, where others find theirs later in life, but the important thing is that you use it or them to glorify God. There are also people who are naturally good at everything and go back and forth in between things never mastering their true passion.

Jesus said "to one he gave five talents, to another two, and to another, one – to each according to his own ability" (Matthew 25:15a HCSB).

When you tap into your talent and develop them with a passion, they can lead you beyond your wildest dreams.

PERSONAL PRAYER TIME

"But we will devote ourselves to prayer"
(Acts 6:4 HCSB).

I t is a great privilege and honor to be able to approach the throne of God in prayer. In Old Testament times, believers had to go to the high priest in order to be heard by God and receive God's instruction, wisdom, help, encouragement and guidance. Today we have our Lord and Savior Jesus Christ to cast our cares upon (1 Peter 5:7). Where there are various prayers such as: corporate, warfare, prayers of thanksgiving, protection, provision and prayers of intercession, to name a few. The pattern and responsibility remains the same.

When we enter into our sacred place of prayer we first must approach the Father through His Son Jesus (John 16:23b). Next, you must enter into prayer with the attitude of worship, and the expectation to meet and commune with God and surrender your will in order to permit God's will to be done! Whether your prayer will be answered now, later, or in a matter that you didn't expect. His will must be done. By surrendering you also acknowledge that you fully trust and rely on God to the fullest. Even if God's will is not to grant your request at that moment or way you must trust that all things will still work together for your good! (Romans 8:28).

In prayer you must also seek to know and understand the Will of God. Remember, prayer is a two way conversation with the Lord, so you must listen for an answer and pray back what the Lord said to you. This unifies your desires with His divine will and builds maturity and cultivates your faith. Ask for your physical needs and make your request known unto God. This is the time to truly pour out to Him from your heart.

While you're in private prayer this will be your time to pray in the Spirit to build up your spirit man (Romans 8:26). While in your prayer closet Christ has instructed us to pray for the advancement of the Kingdom (Matthew 9:38). If you're in corporate prayer the word says to

> By surrendering you also acknowledge that you fully trust and rely on God to the fullest.

first confess your sins and concerns to one another, then pray for each other (James 5:16).

I believe that one of the first and most essential elements of powerful, pure prayer is true repentance (Matthew 6:12-13). This is because your prayers will be hindered because of the presence and existence of sin in your life, and strife between spouses (Isaiah 59:2, Romans 3:23, 1 Peter 3:7).

(Matthew 6:7-8) warns us not to pray for show in order to be seen or thought of as powerful and anointed. Pray from and with a sincere heart even if your words are not elegant and smooth because God already knows what you need before you ask.

For this reason, believers must be taught what to pray and not just how to pray (Luke 11:11) by the Holy Spirit.

Pray in expectancy, enthusiastically, purely, and persistently (Luke 11:5-10). As you begin to follow this pattern of prayer in whatever setting you are in, you will not only start to see results and receive answers, but you will truly start falling in love with prayer. "The intense prayer of the Righteous is very powerful" (James 5:16 HCSB). Remember that nothing leaves heaven until prayer leaves earth!

YOUR INTERCESSIONS

"The Lord said: assuredly, I will set you free and care for you.
Assuredly, I will intercede for you in a time of trouble, in your
time of distress, with the enemy"
(Jeremiah 15:11 HCSB)

To intercede is to stand in the spiritual gap with and for someone. Intercessory prayer is often associated with spiritual warfare. But, it can also be when you are in agreement for a breakthrough or miracle, or when you are praying for protection and for God to build and sustain His people (Ephesians 6:18-19). Intercessory prayer is vital in the building and up keeping of the Kingdom of God.

"He saw that there was no man – He was amazed that there was no one interceding, so His own arm brought salvation, and His own righteousness supported Him" (Isaiah 59:16 HCSB).

As believers we've been entrusted with the great privilege and responsibility to pray for one another as Christ intercedes for us (John 17, Romans 8:34). As you enter into the presence of God on the behalf of someone else and all of the believers, you will start to see God moving on your behalf without you even asking. This is true Kingdom work because the King Himself became a sacrifice unto the world, so you should sacrifice your prayers on the behalf of the world. You may have a co-worker, neighbor, friend, or family member that doesn't know Christ as their personal Savior. Stand in the gap and plead on their behalf that God removes their stony heart and implant a heart of flesh.

The perfect example will be found in Exodus chapters 5-14 where Moses became a mighty liaison and intercessor between the stubborn Pharaoh and the oppressed Israelites. Moses stayed persistent in his time spent with the Father, the Israelites and Pharaoh until Israel's breakthrough came. There is a difference between intercessory prayer and the office of an intercessor, but every believer and especially leaders have the task of going to God on the behalf of others (Matthew 9:38, James 5:16).

Intercessory prayer does require discipline and may even call for some tarrying in the Spirit. But it is an awesome responsibility that every believer has and must be understood and managed properly with the right spirit and attitude. Sometimes God will drop someone into your spirit during your normal daily routine or you may be asleep and the Spirit will awaken you during your midnight hour to stand in on someone's behalf. Don't take this lightly because someone, somewhere is in need of your prayers. "First of all, then, I urge that petitions, prayers, intercessions

> As believers we've been entrusted with the great privilege and responsibility to pray for one another as Christ intercedes for us (see John 17, Romans 8:34).

and thanksgivings be made for everyone, for kings and all those who are in authority, so that we may lead a tranquil and quiet life in all goodness and dignity.

This is good, and it pleases God our Savior, who wants everyone to be saved and to come to the knowledge of the truth" (1 Timothy 2:1-4 HCSB). If you want to see the awesome power of God, stand in the gap today for someone else!

OTHER BELIEVERS

"Now, finally, all of you should be like-minded and sympathetic, should love believers, and be compassionate and humble, not paying back evil for evil or insult for insult but, on the contrary, giving a blessing, since you were called for this, so that you can inherit a blessing"

(1 Peter 3:8-9 HCSB).

I once heard a touching story about a man who would come to church Sunday after Sunday and his shoes would be completely dusty. There was an irritated and upset mother in the church that began to criticize the old man, saying things such as: "Why can't he at least clean his shoes before coming to church? Or his house has to be dirty, because your appearance says a lot about who you are." She'd also make comments like, "he can't see how nice everyone else looks? What's wrong with him?"

I'm sure you know people like this mother as I do. As the story goes, one day this mother just couldn't take it anymore so she mustered up enough strength and courage after service to approach the old man. As she went to him he hugged her and tears began to flow from his eyes. As she embraced the man he began to tell her how much the service touched him and how he appreciated all the love that has been showed to him.

As they sat down together he began to share with her that after his wife died of cancer two years prior after thirty years of marriage, he lost all hope and gave up on life. He even lost everything he had except his home because of his inability to work due to his depression. One day as he sat on his porch some people from the church invited him to church service and told him about how Jesus loved him. The next Sunday he went to church and accepted Christ as his personal Savior and now he has new life and hope. He then stated that he walks three miles from home and runs late most Sundays because of his bad leg. He has to walk down a dirt road and he said his shoes start off clean and are dirty after the long painful journey.

He told her that he feels bad about it but that the people seem to not notice and they love him anyway and that no one since his wife has loved him so deeply. This made the mother begin to cry also and they became great friends from that day forward.

> Believers have the responsibility of caring for one another and truly expressing the love of God through actions and words of affirmation

Believers have the responsibility of caring for one another and truly expressing the love of God through actions and words of affirmation. see (1 John 4:7) Even when you see your brother or sister stumble and fall don't criticize them but restore them in love because we all fall short of God's glory (2 Timothy 2:24-26). The Apostles were sent out in pairs of two because where one was weak the other was strong, so they balanced each other, and were able to say encouraged (Proverbs 27:17).

New converts need and most often want more mature believers to help assimilate them into the body and help them grow and mature, while understanding their transitional struggles. Become and remain a believer who believes in believers.

EVANGELISM

"To be a minister of Christ Jesus to the Gentiles, serving as a priest of god's good news" (Romans 15:16a HCSB).

A s a young boy growing up the phrase "practice what you preach" seemed to be very common and prominent. Now as an adult and minister, I believe the phrase is very inadequate and is in reverse order while striving in the spirit of excellence. My personal phrase and belief is to preach what you practice. Whether you are a layman or a leader, we all must minister or spread the good news about our loving Father. More often than any, most will find that the true word will hit you before and while ministering to others.

This is because the Bible states, "for the word of God is living and effective and sharper than any two-edged sword, penetrating as far as to divide soul, spirit, joints and marrow; it is a judge of the ideas and thoughts of the heart" (Hebrews 4:12 HCSB).

Another way of putting it is, before you can effectively give a word, you must be living that word because nothing is hidden from God (see verses 13-16). Is this to say that you will be perfect? No, of course not! This is to say that you must make every effort to live life with a clear conscience and strive for perfection before God. You will have a clear conscience once you keep in sync with the precious Spirit of God (Galatians 5:24-25).

Take note of this, "Knowing, then, the fear of the Lord, we persuade people. We are completely open before God, and I hope we are completely open to your consciences as well" (2 Corinthians 5:11 HCSB). Ministering to others is of the utmost importance, but there is another type of ministering that is often overlooked and neglected.

This is called self-ministry. At one point or another you have been down, facing depression, stressed and beat down by life (2 Corinthians 6:4-10). Self-ministry is often referred to as self-encouragement. You may have to get away from people and start talking to yourself sometimes and tell yourself that things will get better, there is hope! You may have to have a praise and worship break, or you may have to do as I do and go into your Bible and find stories of others who have been through similar and worse situations. Read these stories out loud to see how God brought them out to renew your faith and spirit man.

You may have to sing a song, or praying in tongues to build up your spirit man

> Another way of putting it is, before you can effectively give a word, you must be living that word because nothing is hidden from God.

(1 Corinthians 14:4) but you must speak to yourself in order to minister to your storm. You have the right to speak life and new life into yourself. You don't always need to call someone, or get a prayer partner, because you can approach the throne of grace to receive help in your critical time of need (Hebrews 4:16).

You can begin to release your breakthrough and praise God in advance because you know that nothing is based on what it looks like nor how you feel, but on how you know that God will deliver! You must minister to yourself and receive deliverance before you can teach others about it. Remember "greater is He that is in you, than he that is in the world" (1 John 4:4 KJV). To minister, is to spread the good news, even to yourself.

<u>YOUR FORGIVENESS</u>

"And when ye stand praying, forgive, if ye ought against any:
that your Father also which is in heaven may forgive you your
trespasses. But if ye do not forgive, neither will your Father
which is in heaven forgive your trespasses"
(Mark 11:25-26 KJV).

The scripture above says it all in the sense of the pattern of forgiveness. God created man in his own image and likeness, then man became disobedient unto Him and His commands. From that point on a sacrifice of blood had to be made to atone for the forgiveness of sin. Jesus paid the ultimate price for man's sin with His own blood and body during His crucifixion on Mt. Calvary. Believer's must follow the example of Christ in setting other's free from the wrongs that have been done to them by exercising the power of forgiveness.

You not only release others from their wrongs, but you also release yourself from the outcome of the wrong. As well as your involvement in it, and the pain and hurt of the wrong.

Satan has tapped into this pattern of power and tries to hold anger, self-pity, regret, shame, hurt, confusion, and resentment within you while injecting rejection into you. Hoping that you will not and cannot forgive yourself and others. When you fail to forgive you deny the forgiving power of God, so you can never become healed, delivered, whole and free. Harboring unforgiveness also aborts your ability to hear from the Lord so you can't receive His strategies concerning the situation. You, nor the people involved within it.

This is hurtful to all because God wants to be involved in every facet of your life and delights in the outpouring of words of knowledge and words of wisdom to His elect. Harboring unforgiveness is like you shooting yourself with the expectation of killing your antagonist. It's ludicrous because unforgiveness may slightly affect others but, hanging on to it only kills you!

The Apostle Matthew states, "therefore if thou bring thy gift to the altar, and there rememberest that thy brother hath ought against thee; leave there thy gift before the altar, and go thy way; first be reconciled to thy brother, and then come and offer thy gift". (Matthew 5:23-24 KJV).

What Jesus was saying in today's terms is: before you talk to me, start by forgiving yourself and others, then come back and we can talk. It's Satan's job to try to bind and keep you bound, so you can't live in victorious freedom but, it's your job to get free and remain free.

> When you fail to forgive you deny the forgiving power of God, so you can never become healed, delivered, whole and free.

Too many believers are enslaved to their own selves, situations, and circumstances when Christ has freed them. You can and will never know the true love of God until you release yourself from you! Even when you forgive others you must not only forgive but also release the pain and hurt of the problem.

Then you must rebuke the foreign voices that speak within your mind trying to convince you to relive the problem. You must refuse to be held hostage as a victim of offense. Just as God forgives, you must forgive!

Today, I encourage you that if you are holding on to anything tied to unforgiveness, loose yourself! Don't make excuses of it being too hard or people don't understand what happened, or how bad it hurts. The only way for hurt to heal is to face the problem head on and deal with it. Forgiveness is the medicine that releases blessings that must be experienced to be believed such as love, renewed relationships, joy, salvation, and peace just to name a few.

Even though you forgive someone and are forgiven, remember that forgiveness doesn't eradicate consequence. For instance, if a man commits adultery, his wife may forgive him but he still may face the reality of divorce. No matter what the outcome of the offense, you must free yourself because forgiveness releases the abundant life of freedom.

YOUR MATERIAL POSSESSIONS

"But thou shalt remember the Lord thy God: for it is he that giveth thee power to get wealth, that he may establish his covenant which he sware unto thy fathers, as it is this day" (Deuteronomy 8:18 KJV).

Homes, cars, boats, jewelry and fine clothes are all rewards from the Father for your hard work and diligence. Even the unbeliever is rewarded for His work in a natural sense (Psalms 73:12). God wants His people to live in comfort, but with a heavenly perspective at all times. God has blessed you to bless others, not to hoard and showcase your wealth and become consumed by the status quo.

In (Luke 16:19-31) you will find the story of a rich man with the wrong perspective on things. In today's terms the story would go like this: There was a rich man (you can name him) who lived an extremely lavish and flamboyant lifestyle. He drove the latest luxury cars and SUVs, he lived in the biggest and most luxurious mansion in the city and partied with only the most prominent people around. One day some people were watching this guy on television and thought, "this guy could really help our friend Lazarus who's not only poor, but is sick. So they all jumped into their truck and drove thirty minutes to the rich man's home, rung the bell at the gate and left Lazarus there.

This man saw old Lazarus at his gate through his surveillance system and demanded that he leave before he called the cops. But Lazarus didn't leave. He refused to believe that this was the same guy on television that was recognized as a great humanitarian, would turn him away so the rich man put his highly trained k-9s on Lazarus, but God stepped in and the dogs began to lick and sooth the sores on him. The man became furious and said "I won't give you anything!" Can you believe this? A multimillionaire that wouldn't even feed someone?

This happens daily and more often than not, it happens to everyday people. People will get that new car that they've been sowing seeds for and praying for and as soon as they get it they refuse to give someone a ride to the store or church. God wants you to enjoy your riches and even take care of them, but not to become consumed by them and they become your god.

The author of Hebrews states: "Let brotherly love continue. Don't neglect to show hospitality, for by doing this some have welcomed angels as guests without knowing it" (Hebrews 13:1-2 HCSB).

To be a good steward over material things is to use everything you have for the glory of God and advancement of His Kingdom here on Earth (Matthew 25:35-36). I'm not saying give everything away but be guided

> To be a good steward over material things is to use everything you have for the glory of God and advancement of His Kingdom here on Earth.

by and sensitive to the Spirit on who, when and how to help others. After all, you're a manager which means it all belongs to the Father anyway!

By investing in others you will yield tremendous dividends in Heaven and in the lives of others (Luke 6:38 HCSB).

CONCLUSION

"A person should consider us in this way: as servants of Christ and managers of God's mysteries. In this regard, it is expected of managers that each one be found faithful"

(1 Corinthians 4:1-2 HCSB).

I pray that you've not only enjoyed this book, but you've grown in every arena of your life. Becoming a good steward over everything God has entrusted to you is a life-long process and since you've taken the time to read this you're on the road to great biblical stewardship. God has strategically designed perfect patterns for our lives to manage and when we do, the rewards are tremendous.

Continue to seek and pray for ways for God to teach you and strengthen you in your quest to become the best faithful steward you can be to your fullest potential. Be blessed, and enjoy your journey.

About the Author

Burnell Williams, Jr. was born August 10, 1982 in Atlanta, GA. He is the second oldest of six children. He is the devoted husband of Alicia Williams, who is the founder of Divinely Designed Ladies ©. You can also connect with her at livebydivinedesign.com. He also has two daughters, Azariah and Micaela.

He accepted his call into the ministry in January of 2011 and has been determined to spread the gospel and build godly families ever since. He can be contacted via e-mail www.burnellwilliamsjr.com, you can follow him on Twitter @burnell_jr and also connect with him on Facebook: Elder Burnell Williams Jr.